short
steps
for
long
gains

brief studies for
Christian growth

by Simon
Manchester

❀ MATTHIAS MEDIA

Short Steps for Long Gains
© Matthias Media, 2003.
St Matthias Press Ltd. ACN 067 558 365

Distributed in the United Kingdom by:
The Good Book Company
Tel: 0845-225-0880
Fax: 0845-225-0990
Email: admin@thegoodbook.co.uk
Internet: www.thegoodbook.co.uk

ISBN 1 876326 53 0

Cover design and typesetting by Joy Lankshear Design.

Introduction

THIS SMALL BOOKLET has been written to provide a focus for Christians who meet together briefly and regularly to look at God's word, pray and share something of their lives.

It is designed to be done quickly, with a focus on the practical application of biblical truth. Obviously, these verses and questions can't provide all the biblical input that a growing Christian requires. However, they can keep you going, making short steps forward in Christian growth, for long-term gain. In this sense, it is an introductory A to Z of Christian living.

Each verse is chosen so as to focus on the topic for the reflection. However, if you have more time, it will be beneficial to read more than the single verse listed.

The studies work best if one or more of the people meeting has already thought about the answers to the questions, and considered the Bible verse in more detail.

There are twenty-six topics, so the booklet will provide

weekly reflections for half a year, or a year's fortnightly input.

The Bible verses are from the English Standard Version unless otherwise indicated.

Simon Manchester

Assurance

"I write these things to you who believe in the name of the Son of God that you may know that you have eternal life." 1 JOHN 5:13

- What must a person do to have eternal life?
  Believe in the name of the Son of God

- Do you have eternal life?
  Yes

- How do you know you are going to heaven?
  Because I believe in the name of the Son of God

- What is the difference between hoping and knowing?
  Knowing = certain it will happen   hoping = it may

- Is it possible to be secure but not feel it?
  Yes

- Is it possible to feel it but not be secure?
  Yes

- How would you help a Christian who was uncertain of his or her standing before God?

Bible

"All Scripture is breathed out by God and profitable for teaching, for reproof, for correction, and for training in righteousness..." 2 TIMOTHY 3:16

❯ What does 'breathed out by God' mean?

❯ What does 'all Scripture' mean?

❯ Why are the four functions (above) all necessary?

❯ How do you organize your reading?

❯ What Bible reading methods do you know?

❯ Are you making excuses for not reading the Bible?

❯ Why is daily reading a good goal?

Christ

"I want to know Christ and the power of his resurrection and the fellowship of sharing in his sufferings..." PHILIPPIANS 3:10 (NIV)

- ◉ Does Paul know Christ or not?

- ◉ Can power and suffering go together?

- ◉ Which sufferings can we share in?

- ◉ Which sufferings can we not share in?

- ◉ Do you desire to 'know Christ better'?

- ◉ Do you think of Christ as a 'living' friend?

- ◉ What helps and hinders the friendship?

Discipleship

"The Son of Man must suffer many things...and be killed, and on the third day be raised...If anyone would come after me, let him deny himself and take up his cross daily and follow me." LUKE 9:22-23

- What is the difference between Jesus' cross and ours?

- Why is following Jesus (discipleship) so difficult?

- What sort of denial does Jesus mean?

- In practice, how do we take up our cross?

- In what areas do disciples struggle the most?

- Which areas are hardest for you?

- Is the 'following' worth it? Why?

Evangelism

"All authority in heaven and on earth has been given to me. Go therefore and make disciples of all nations...And behold, I am with you always, to the end of the age."

MATTHEW 28:18-20

- How does Jesus have such authority?

- How might we explain it to a sceptic?

- What does the command 'make disciples' mean?

- What power creates a new disciple?

- What makes a mature disciple?

- Who will Christ be 'with'?

- How are you going as a witness to Jesus?

Fellowship

"And let us consider how to stir up one another to love and good works, not neglecting to meet together, as is the habit of some, but encouraging one another..."

HEBREWS 10:24-25

- ▶ Why is meeting together important?

- ▶ What might keep you from 'meeting'?

- ▶ How do bad habits in this area affect us?

- ▶ How do bad habits in this area affect others?

- ▶ What factors bring about good fellowship?

- ▶ Who encourages you?

- ▶ Can you improve your effectiveness in encouraging others?

Growth

"But grow in the grace and knowledge of our Lord and Saviour Jesus Christ."

2 PETER 3:18

- What is 'grace' for Christians?

- How do you learn more of his grace?

- Is 'knowledge' just intellectual?

- Who do you know who is 'growing'?

- Have you been growing this year?

- What has contributed to that?

- Are there any incentives to grow?

Home

"And whatever you do, in word or deed, do everything in the name of the Lord Jesus, giving thanks to God the Father through him." COLOSSIANS 3:17

- How is the gospel affecting your home life?

- Does this verse allow for the separation of 'Christian' and 'secular' life?

- How do we do things in Jesus' name?

- Is anything outside his interest?

- What makes this command hard to keep at your place?

- Could you really change things?

- How could your home be more fruitful?

Income

"On the first day of every week, each of you should set aside a sum of money in keeping with his income..." 1 CORINTHIANS 16:2 (NIV)

- How much of your money belongs to God?

- How much should we give to gospel work?

- Which words above imply discipline?

- What guidance is provided concerning the amount to give?

- What benefits come from generosity?

- What is the greatest incentive to generosity?

- How is your giving going?

Joy

"Nevertheless, do not rejoice in this, that the spirits are subject to you, but rejoice that your names are written in heaven."

LUKE 10:20

> Why does Jesus warn against spiritual success?

> Why does experience make a poor foundation for assessing ourselves spiritually?

> Is Jesus announcing a ban or a warning?

> What is the real basis for joy?

> Is rejoicing 'in the Lord' always possible?

> Do you rejoice much or little?

> How can you increase your joy?

ingdom

"...seek first the kingdom of God and his righteousness, and all these things will be added to you." MATTHEW 6:33

- How does a non-Christian seek God's kingdom?

- How does a Christian seek it?

- Where do we see Christ's kingdom/government?

- Why does this priority liberate us?

- Does this priority make your work suffer?

- What 'things' does Jesus promise to provide?

- How can you put his kingdom 'first'?

Loneliness

"At my first defence no one came to stand
by me, but all deserted me. But the Lord
stood by me and strengthened me..."

2 TIMOTHY 4:16-17

- Do you have some close friends?

- Can you share deep things with anyone?

- Are people lonely by their own fault or not?

- Was Paul a lonely person? Why or why not?

- How close is your fellowship with Christ?

- What does God give to prevent loneliness?

- How can you improve your friendships?

arriage

"...let each one of you love his wife as himself, and let the wife see that she respects her husband." EPHESIANS 5:33

- What is the goal of marriage?

- Is marriage a painful issue for you? Why/why not?

- How is a husband supposed to 'love'?

- How important are feelings in marriage?

- How is a wife supposed to show 'respect'?

- Do you and your partner share in spiritual matters (e.g. pray together)?

- How can you deepen your marriage?

ormality

"In this world you will have trouble.
But take heart! I have overcome the world."

JOHN 16:33 (NIV)

- How does Jesus' realistic outlook help us?

- What troubles have surprised you lately?

- Is the 'trouble' for Christians or for anyone?

- What inward troubles disappoint you?

- In what sense has Jesus 'overcome the world'?

- How does this give us 'heart'?

- How can we show 'heart' in 'trouble'?

Opposition

"Your adversary the devil prowls around like a roaring lion...Resist him, firm in your faith..." **1 PETER 5:8-9**

❯ What are the common roles of the devil?

❯ Why is he 'your adversary'?

❯ How do we know he is real?

❯ How do we know he can be beaten?

❯ When have you had to resist?

❯ What faith makes us firm?

❯ How does Jesus suggest we pray? (see Matthew 6:13)

rayer

"Pray then like this: Our Father in heaven..." MATTHEW 6:9

- Why is the 'Lord's Prayer' a great gift to us?

- What do you notice about the order of the prayer?

- Do you find time to pray daily?

- How is prayer with your wife/husband/friends going?

- What do you find hardest in prayer?

- Have you had remarkable answers to prayer?

- How can we improve church prayer?

Questions

"Are you the one who is to come, or shall we look for another?" LUKE 7:19

- Why is John the Baptist unsure about whom Jesus is?

- When is such questioning healthy?

- When is it unhealthy?

- What faith issues have you questioned lately?

- Which books have helped your faith?

- Can doubt strengthen faith? In what ways?

- Are you strengthening your faith? Why or why not?

Rules

"So then, the law was our guardian until Christ came, in order that we might be justified by faith." GALATIANS 3:24

- ❯ How was the law our 'guardian'?

- ❯ In what way does Christ rescue us?

- ❯ What happens when Christians live by rules?

- ❯ Does this mean the law is gone?

- ❯ Do you lean toward 'law' or 'faith' in your attitude to life?

- ❯ How can we be free from rules?

- ❯ How does faith bring obedience?

ex

"For the one who sows to his own flesh will from the flesh reap corruption, but the one who sows to the Spirit will from the Spirit reap eternal life." GALATIANS 6:8

- ❯ What two fields for sowing lie before a Christian?

- ❯ Why are these unique to Christians?

- ❯ What harvest comes from disobedience?

- ❯ What harvest comes from obedience?

- ❯ How does God help us in this struggle?

- ❯ Where are the subtlest dangers?

- ❯ How is your sexual faithfulness going?

Temptation

"Then Jesus was led up by the Spirit into the wilderness to be tempted by the devil."

MATTHEW 4:1

- Was Jesus in the wrong to be tempted?

- How can Spirit-led living bring temptation?

- Where did the devil strike Jesus? (see Matthew 4:1-11)

- How did Jesus strengthen his resolve?

- Does his victory really help us?

- Why is our failure not final?

- How can we be more victorious?

Usefulness

"Therefore, if anyone cleanses himself from what is dishonourable, he will be a vessel for honourable use, set apart as holy, useful to the master of the house, ready for every good work." 2 TIMOTHY 2:21

- How do you sense God has used you?

- Who around you seems to be greatly used by God?

- Where would you like to be useful?

- What may hinder your usefulness?

- List three ways you can be useful today.

- Is there a ministry for you in your church?

- How can you do things that are useful for eternity?

ision

"Look, I tell you, lift up your eyes, and see that the fields are white for harvest." JOHN 4:35

- ◐ What 'fields' is Jesus talking about?

- ◐ Where around you is there a harvest without workers?

- ◐ Where around you is Christian witness weak?

- ◐ How can we play a part (be it small but real)?

- ◐ Whose Christian vision lifts yours?

- ◐ Do you have any ideas for your church to work on?

- ◐ How are we hindered from fulfilling our vision?

ork

"Whatever you do, work heartily, as for the Lord and not for men..." COLOSSIANS 3:23

- Do you love or loathe your work?

- Would you consider yourself a workaholic?

- Where do you get your identity?

- What are you like on holidays?

- How can we really work 'for the Lord'?

- Are you prepared to lose money for Christ's sake?

- What makes Christian workers different?

eercise

"...for while bodily training is of some value, godliness is of value in every way, as it holds promise for the present life and also for the life to come." 1 TIMOTHY 4:8

- ❯ How does exercise give value?

- ❯ What exercise do you try to do, physical and spiritual?

- ❯ Is 'godliness' hard work?

- ❯ Does it come passively or actively?

- ❯ Why is it good in the 'present'?

- ❯ Why is it good in 'the life to come'?

- ❯ How can we balance the hours spent on different kinds of exercise?

esterday

"Forgetting what lies behind and straining forward to what lies ahead, I press on toward the goal for the prize of the upward call of God in Christ Jesus." PHILIPPIANS 3:13-14

- ❯ How can we forget 'what lies behind'?

- ❯ What are we tempted to remember?

- ❯ What is Paul tempted to remember?

- ❯ Which past issues are important?

- ❯ Why do we get bogged down?

- ❯ Do you really press on toward the heavenly goal?

- ❯ What can we do to increase our hope?

Zeal

"Do not be slothful in zeal, be fervent in spirit, serve the Lord." ROMANS 12:11

- Is zeal an action or a feeling or something else?

- How does the gospel create zeal?

- How does serving him create zeal?

- When does zeal diminish?

- How is your enthusiasm at the moment?

- Who lifts your spiritual enthusiasm?

- Having finished this booklet, who can you now nurture in zealous faith?

Finished? Try these...

ONE2ONE

ONE2ONE
a resource for Bible-reading partnerships

Many people struggle to maintain a consistency in their Bible reading and prayer. God's solution to our struggles is to give us one another!

This new resource by Andrew Cornes is designed to help people form Bible reading partnerships, where they meet together perhaps once a week to read, discuss and pray through a passage of scripture. The book contains 24 readings on John and Philippians. Suitable for men, women or couples.

ON THE MOVE
Bible readings for people on the go

This is the first of an experimental format for a daily Bible-reading resource for commuters and others who may not have the time for a quiet time at home. It combines the printed text of the passage to be studied with a brief introduction and a couple of questions to ponder and apply. There are also brief suggestions for prayer. Each booklet contains forty readings—enough for two months-worth of train journeys to work!

Call us on 0845 225 0880 or email admin@thegoodbook.co.uk

Who are we?

Ever since we opened our doors in 1991 as St Matthias Press, our aim has been to provide the Christian community with products of a uniformly high standard—both in their biblical faithfulness and in the quality of the writing and production.

Now known as The Good Book Company, we have grown to become an international provider of user-friendly resources, many of them from Matthias Media in Australia, with Christians of all sorts using our Bible studies, books, Briefings, audio cassettes, videos, training courses and daily Bible reading resources.

Buy direct or from your local bookshop

You can order your resources either direct from us, or from your local Christian bookshop. There are advantages in both, but if you buy from us, you get these benefits:

* you save time—we usually despatch our orders within 24 hours of receiving them
* you save money—we have built-in discounts for bulk buying.

Please call us for a free catalogue of all our resources.

| ☎ 0845-225-0880 | ✉ Elm House, 37 Elm Road, New Malden, Surrey KT3 3HB | FAX 0845-225-0990 (pay by credit card or invoice) |

Email: admin@thegoodbook.co.uk
Website: www.thegoodbook.co.uk